DATE DUE			
FEB 22 1993			
JUL 1 5 2003			

THE
LOVE SPACE
DEMANDS
A Continuing Saga

THE LOVE SPACE DEMANDS

A Continuing Saga

NTOZAKE SHANGE

St. Martin's Press
New York

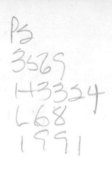

Selected poems from *The Love Space Demands* have appeared in *Uncut Funk, Shooting Star Review, Muleteeth, Konch, Yellow Silk,* and *Real News.*

Production Editor: David Stanford Burr

Design by Glen M. Edelstein

Library of Congress Cataloging-in-Publication Data

Shange, Ntozake.
    The love space demands / Ntozake Shange.
        p.   cm.
    ISBN 0-312-05892-6
    I. Title.
    PS3569.H3324L68 1991
    811'.54—dc20   90-27412
                                                   CIP

First Edition: June 1991

10 9 8 7 6 5 4 3 2 1

for my beaux,

C. L. R. James & Romare Bearden

Contents

I Heard Eric Dolphy In His Eyes

Acknowledgments

These pieces have had myriad lives and nurturers. I must thank Rozlyn Allen for her hospitality; Halima Taha for her arts administration skills; Dianna Houston, Gwen Hardisan, Denise de la Peña, and Pat-Hall Smith for giving powerful voices to Annie and company at a closed reading in SoHo. I must thank Kwame Shaw of Greenwich House for offering us our first home and Richard Toscan, Drama Chair at the University of Southern California, for providing us with a resilient workshop production of "i heard eric dolphy in his eyes." Grateful acknowledgment must go to Leila Hassan and Darcus Howe of Creation-for-Liberation in Brixton who produced a tour of England for me and these poems and were instrumental in assisting the late C.L.R. James to see me and my daughter once more before he left us. Thanks must go to Bob Holman of Poetry Spots as well as Angela Fontanez for the wonderful video production of "Serial Monogamy," to the Painted Bride Art Center in Philadelphia, American-Audio Prose Library and, finally, to Sidne Mahone, Mickey Davidson, and Talvin Wilkes of Crossroads Theater, with whom Billy ("Spaceman") Patterson, Jr., and I have welded all this love & trouble, into something we can handle, while my editor, Michael Denneny, and his assistant, Keith Kahla, insisted there was a book in all this drama.

Ntozake Shange
8 January 1991

Author's Note

The poems in this volume were refined in performance with my band, Syllable: John Purcell (reeds) and Jean-Paul Bourelly (guitar) from 1988 to the present. In addition Rasul Siddik (trumpet), Tyler Mitchell and Don Pate (bass), Ronnie Bourrage (percussion), and Kelvin Bell, (guitar) worked with me at times since 1987. Billy Bang (violinist) composed the score for the workshop production of *I Heard Eric Dolphy in His Eyes* at the University of Southern California. Billy "Spaceman" Patterson, Jr., is the composer and guitarist on "Serial Monogamy." Mickey Davidson, choreographer and dancer, contributed immensely to the full performance of a number of these pieces.

Ntozake Shange
Philadelphia, 1990

The following cassettes, which include a number of pieces from this book, are available:

"Ntozake Shange with Syllable: Live at The Victoria Theater, San Francisco," Spring 1989; from the San

Francisco Poetry Center, San Francisco State
University, 1600 Holloway Avenue, San Francisco,
CA, 14132.

"Beneath the Necessity of Talking," Ntozake Shange
Live with Syllable, Spring, 1989. Recorded at The
Painted Bride, American Audio Prose Library, P.O.
Box 842, Columbia, MO, 65205.

"Serial Monogamy," video performance for WNYC-
TV by Ntozake Shange and Billy "Spaceman"
Patterson, December, 1989. Contact Bob Holman
WNYC, 1 Centre Street, New York, NY, 10007.

Introduction

After two weeks struggling with writing an introduction to *The Love Space Demands* and *I Heard Eric Dolphy in His Eyes* I headed off to my Women's Meeting with desperation. There I confessed that I was having trouble writing about love poems I myself had created, plus I was confusing them with a collection of black erotica I was to review. I begged for assistance. Watching the women in my group suppress giggles, raise eyebrows, and wiggle in their seats, I realized that we all were having trouble separating love from sex, sensuality from affection, devotion from masochism, and independence from fear of intimacy. I hurried from the meeting to get a very rare hamburger from an express-gourmet-deli near a truck stop in my neighborhood. In other words, to rid myself of the anticipatory "rush" I was experiencing from single-minded attention to my visions of lust and love, I took myself someplace familiar, but rarefied, to indulge in raw pleasure. I could not scoop up an adequate lover or boyfriend or sex partner or companion or intimate (I am reluctant to make a choice even about what the person is), but in the absence of such a counterpart, I ate alla this hamburger. I don't eat red meat much, but then, a luscious love (romantic or sensual episode), is, also, singular.

The epiphany of orgasms or infatuations is a consistently sought after reward for leading an otherwise reasonable life. But the transmissions of sexual diseases, including AIDS, now associated with such coming together weighs heavily on choices baby-boomers had come to make with leisure. Now, sex-death is not a Victorian metaphor for chastity. Sex-death has given birth to a whole new slew of epithets and lines meant to get somebody something they wanted, regardless of the threat to the integrity of language or love. So, monogamy is tossed around like a football or a college freshman at a frat party gone mad. Women who seek to fullfill their own sexual and sensual requisites are, again, sluts and loose. Unwanted children and pregnancies blight relationships and lives, leaving women and men baffled and angry with one another.

Our behaviors were just beginning to change when the epidemic began, moving sex closer to shame now than any time since I've been alive. Words and attitudes that undermine trust and liberty to feel are creeping back into the bedrooms and couches of our lives, so that we are always second-guessing each other. When that fails, the artificial highs of cocaine, crack, methamphetamine, heroin, alcohol, compulsive sex or compulsive suffering come sauntering down the street and into our vacant, yearning lives. The sanctity of an inner quiet and clarity present in the spirit is the least that opening up to another person requires. When we don't know what we mean or why we are doing what we do, we are only able to bring chaos and pain to ourselves and others.

I didn't know what was being said to me, sometimes. Sometimes, I couldn't fathom why any of us were doing what we were doing and calling ourselves somebody's beloved. The poems and monologues in *The Love Space Demands* and *I Heard Eric Dolphy in His Eyes* are real questions I have asked and the sharp edges of the answers.

The Promise/ The Premise

This poem was written in response to Robert Mapplethorpe's photographs of black men/ to be used at his request as an introduction to his *Black Book.*

irrepressibly bronze, beautiful & mine

i.

all my life they've been near me
these men/
    some for a while like the
friend of my father's who drove
each summer from denver to
st. louis/ with some different
white woman/ i remember one seemed
to like me/ she had rose blond hair
i wondered/ why do you like me
you're with him & he's mine
he's colored/ he'll always be
like that/ like me/ i think
he knew my eight-year-old
precocious soul was hankering
for days to come with one/
one of them colored fellas
who'd be mine/ on purpose/ not
just cause of some pigmentation
problem/ or a grandfather clause
in mississippi/ i lived there near
the water/ the river/ the silt
caking my calves/ me laughin with
the younguns/ the boys who'd be
black men one day
        if they lived so long

he brought me rocks/ each sojourn
quartz marble granite & sandstone

onyx ovals i could hold onto when
he drove off with the white woman
i never felt sad/ i didn't know i might
be experiencing rejection/ a little
colored girl with an ebony stone
in the palm of her hand
i knew that was his heart
where could a man go without his heart
a child by the mississippi grasping
dreams/ yet to grab holto a man
but nighttime & motown asked me to dance
sang sweet streams of sweat
moist kisses/ those arrogant torsos
daring crackers or a fool to
look the wrong way/ no just look
a funny way & it'd be over
or just begun

look at me pretty niggah

bring it over here/ i'm grown
now & the stones don't sit
static in my hand/ you know
how it is black volcanoes erupt
they say when miles davis manages
to whisper/ they erupt they say
when the blackstone rangers take
a stroll/ black volcanoes seep
lava anywhere there's true love
now i'm not talkin about
a hoot and holler or a dance on a dime
but whenever there's true
love/ black volcanoes seep lava
& it's always been mine

always my dear like the Bible
says an eye for an eye/ there's
a me for a you

     bring it on baby
i've been holding your heart in
my hand since i was a child
i've been preoccupied on occasion
     but i had to grow some too
cause i wanted what all you were
what all you are/ now you're a man
you've got the world watchin your
every move/ i've got your heart
& by the mississippi/ when i was a
   child/ we callt that a groove
sweet black-eyed pea
honey dripped husk

   bring it on/ i'm not afraid

i've known you all my life
    & this my dear is just the
beginning
the first inkling of what they're gonna
     hear
it ain't no lie that we could sing
don't be embarrassed/ just appear
right there
    the way i have you/ those
times you're brown & wet/ those
times your strength can't be met
just be
   &
remember me/ oh back then

when you rode off & left
   your heart in the palm
      of my child hand

ii.

he's of course george jackson
doing push-ups and visiting with angela

soledad   soledad

confined to his beauty alone
fighting cement walls for air
malcolm's last breath king's crumbling torso
speak to me of beauty
blood beauty courage sweating rage
of course he's lumumba
see only the eyes/ bob marley wail
in the night ralph featherstone
burning temples as pages of books
become ashen and smolder by his ankles
walter rodney's blood fresh soakin
the streets/ leon damas spoke poems
with this face/ césaire cursed our
enemies/ making welcome our true voice
the visage of a people
continually mourning
recognized our beauty so slowly
our heroes fade like jackie wilson
in silence/ in the still of the night

soledad mi amor soledad

iii.

among palms whistling lizards
nestle by roots freshly humid
roots by palm fronds the sun
tickles lovers inviting them to
make quickly some love in
moist sands seeping through toes
pull down the bosom the legs
wiry & thick haired pull down
the petticoats/ lace panties
perfumed lips skipping over
shoulders muscles making music
where before only acacias & macaws
dared solo/ many duets
have been abandoned by the trunks
of palms searching for
moonlight/ rushing toward the sky
as tongues would wrap round
each other/ dew like honey
slipping from their lips
whole skies fallen by
their feet/

    jaguars prowl when their
eyes meet.

The Love Space Demands

even tho yr sampler broke down on you

magnolias & forsythia blossom
from yr Sugar Hill/ Ray Drummond
plays nasty riffs & i imagine
alla the Palm Cafe turns out
when you glow at dusk on
Convent Avenue/ slidin easily by
the just-for-us propositions Gylan Kain
fashioned at every other Harlem corner/
we usedta leave deluxe issues of
love potions/ remedies even insinuations
danglin from Baptist steeples/ Methodist steps
jump back/ jump up/ beatin down/ flyin
yng wenches whose skirts still
tease solos over to the Savoy/

    (you cd make yrself irresistible/ be my
       Willis Avenue Bridge/ floatin/ Rican wet
        su lengua dulce/ over an East River of
          gardenias/ remember the minor sixth)
you hummed to me while I was
reachin for the/ ceilin/ where our
folks was carryin on before Michelangelo
or Lionel Richie/ some where round there
where you brush up gainst baobabs/ well
        (you know where my beauty marks are/ all
over
HARLEM)
we sing like flowers/ i see
round brown honies giggle at us/ the
silly/ niggahness of yr quick light

kisses/ *cómo* fresh/ *mi chabalo negro*/ *mi propio* Tito
Puente/
    my own rhythmn section/ that petal
  openin evey time yr lips/ let
love/ *cada vez*/ yr lips
let love fall/ all
over
Sugar Hill

serial monogamy

i think/ we should reexamine/ serial monogamy
is it/ one at a time or
one for a long time?
                          how
does the concept of infinity relate to a skilled
serial monogamist/ & can
that person consider a diversionary escapade
a serial
one night stand?
                    can a consistent
serial monogamist
have one/ several/ or myriad relationships
that broach every pore of one's body
   so long as there is no penetration?
do we/ consider adventurous relentless tongues
capable of penetration & if we do
can said tongues whip thru us indiscriminately
with words/ like

                          "hello"
   "oh, you lookin good"
   "you jigglin, baby"
cd these be reckless immature violations of
serial monogamy?

   i mean/
if my eyes light up cuz
   some stranger just lets go/ caint stop hisself
from sayin
             "yr name must be paradise"
      if i was to grin or tingle/ even get a lil happy/

      hearin me & paradise/ now synonyms
does that make me a scarlet woman?
      if i wear a red dress that makes someone else hot
      does that put me out the fryin pan & into the
fire?

say/
my jade bracelet got hot
                  (which aint possible cuz jade aint
jade
                  if it aint cold)
but say
my jade got lit up & burst offa my wrist
& i say/
            "i gotta find my precious stones
cuz they my luck"
                  & he say
"luck don't leave it goes where
you need it"
            & i say
"i gotta find my bracelet"
                  & he say
"you know for actual truth
                  you was wearin this bracelet?"
& i say
   "a course, it's my luck"
                  & he say
"how you know?"
& i say
      "cuz
      i heard my jade
      flyin thru the air
      over yr head

            behind my knees
            &
            up under the Japanese lampshade!"
                & he say
"you heard yr jade flyin thru the air?"
            "yes"
                    i say
"& where were they flyin from"
                he say
        "from my arm" i say
        "they got hot & jumped offa my arm"
"but/
where was yr arm?"
                    he say
& i caint say mucha nothin
cuz
where my arm was a part a some tremendous
current/
cd be 'lectricity or niggahs on fire/
so where my arm was is where/ jade gets hot
& does that imply the failure of serial monogamy?

do flamin flyin jade stones
on a arm/ that is a kiss/ & a man who knows where/
luck is
take the serial/ outta monogamy/ & leave
love?

intermittent celibacy

listenin to bobby timmons & jackie wilson
does not encourage abstinence/
& it's not like smokey misled me/ either/
i cdn't get nobody to let me be a bad girl &
how i tried to get one of them/ to make me
a woman/
let me out the deprivations of virginty
                             anna mae wong's fans
                             flutterin
                             over audrey hepburn's shorn
                             head
                             in fronta the cross/
                             Holy Mary Mother of God/
let somebody else come take me/
                             surely
                             The Lord God Almighty
gotta 'nough virgins
to make a rich mullah
forsake Muhammed/
                             (figuratively speaking of
                             course)
all i wanted
was to be/ revealed
& that's what happens to alla us
like/ unto
                             Mary   Isis   Oshun
                             Kali   Ishtar   Tlalozlatl
to leave the sexual covenant
of the   Father
     some other man/ has to make you bleed,
but

it gets better/
there are other fingers tongues loins hair/
everywhere
sweat/ sounds no one's ever heard/ an achin quiet
makes yearnin for salvation/ minor penance
all

this you can/ suffer
all
this/ minglin breath & cum
like the nectar offered on Olympus
from yr tongue to his cheek/ & his
shoulder/ the river niger is flowin/ &
you've fallen/ from
                            Grace
my dear/
you gave it up/ & now
whatchu gonna keep?

                                    memories of inchoate
                              union
                        the mole on his left leg
                  chantin at the ashram
            you say you gave up meat
you thought you were a
      gift of god/
                                    you close yr legs to the flesh
but does that fill you/ with the Holy Ghost?
is/ not runnin off with that pretty
muthafuckah you been hankerin after/
a spirit-filled occasion?
                        if/
you don't allow nobody
to touch you in the bed you share
                        but

the southeastern coast of france
is some/ other/ where you
available?

       can
you touch yrself

       &
when you do/ do you rush to say
"get thee behind me
Satan?"

       or
has/ the devil caressed yr eyebrows
left you/ gaspin
for/ just one mo
temptation?

          is it/ okay/
          to wait a week
          or/ say
          change the sheets?

you know/
it's been a day & a half
  since i had any/
& do any you've had
know you/ that you
a gift of god
& the devil's mistress/

          abstinence
          is not
          celibacy
cuz/ when you filled with the Holy Ghost
every man/ in the world
can smell it/

          you wake up drippin
          with the
          spirit

doves perch by yr clit
cooin with the drifters
til the paragons & the jesters
come/ flyin all they colors
lay claim/ to yr moans
bring you right up to em
with/ the "wind"
oh-oh-oh wind   wind

chastening with honey

by all rites i shd be writin
right to left/ upside down
or backwards/
speech/ shd run garbled & dyslexic thru my
brain/ til i hear yr voice
clearly/ again/

in some other/ life were you a mandala?
are you "OM"?
is shakti-pat/ yr regular metabolic status/
under ordinary circumstances?
oh/ there I go again
admirin myself/ unwittingly/
invitin some terribly/ lush *mot palabra son syllable*/
to flail
abt my bangs & lashes
so moist/ you smile/ i remember/ this is arrogance
& it's over

this/ chastening with honey
is nothin/ like the Passion of Christ/
which brought us Lent & we give up meat/
quit our lust/ for blood & bonbons/
Mohammed's trials brought Ramadan/ & we may only
quench our thirst for life from dawn to dusk/
& Buddha/ neath the bo tree/ spread joy abt our
ankles
so long as we rid ourselves of resentment &
impatience/ now Krishna/ is another kind of story/
but goatherds & goatherdesses/ sheperds &
sheperdesses/
all come with chastening.

you may/ sheer this wool/ wet it
braid it til you can wrap it round/ two or three
parallel/ cosmic strings/
just don't/ disrupt the ritual
the leap from maya to nirvana/ overwhelms
unwitting/ arrogance
& *je ne sais que ton insouciance*/ we
can't handle passion/ with the deftness
we associate with civil servants/ in Ibadan or
Bogota/
i am so lucky
this is the essence of life/ you
present yrself/ with the warmth of the Goddess/
the ferocity of Yahweh/ the glee of Shiva/ the
cunning of Coyote/ the de-groovi-licious breath of
Obatala/ like
there was some difference tween yr voice/ this
honey/ fallin off
my body/ & wild hummingbirds from the rain forest
appear
by the A train/ imaginin you some/ tropical flower
pollen
hoverin over Manhattan/ like the Muslim brother's
incense/
maybe/ if i burn you up/ i'd calm down/
the endorphin crazed
birds/ cd go back to the Amazon/   think abt it/
fire/ is a great rite of passage/   the pollen &
the honey & the
flyin birds by my cheek/ oh oh/ i understand/
this is the fall from the Garden.

a third generation geechee myth for yr birthday

(for John Purcell)

when we fall from the stars to the bellies of
our mothers/ some folks say
        they's music in the air/ dontcha think/
we tumble thru a niggah
night/ etchin light
            thru them black holes
unimaginable density
inconceivable radiance/ black
pitch/ maybe the air
in a black hole/ is the sacred hush of rushes round
lil baby moses/ or might cd be the fire
brightenin black holes/ is reliable
as maceo's wail/ when we glide
from planet to planet/ swing right past our own
down/ to our mothers' bellies
some folks say
        they's a storm a comin/
& the sea belts the shores/ how
ben webster burst thru a eye of a hurricane/
gilmore singin volcanic steam/ fool enough
to rise up from ashes/ molten glowin
            any kinda dead fire
caint/ fly out no niggah night/
        to our mothers' bellies/ caint lead us
outta black hole/ slyly shepp or
prophet ayler/ overwhelming pressure
epistemologically/ impossible constructs/
left bird & dapper lester/ outside kansas city
goin somewhere/ must be/ on our way

cuz/ we done come careenin out severely colored
stratospheres/
surgin with the force of them/ what
am in the tradition/ & them what aint
caint/ smoke cigars or make light in a white hole
either/
be like playin a tenor wit a trumpet
mouthpiece/ mistakin junior walker
for philip glass/ no no no/ that aint our way
when/ we come sailin out the vistas of galaxies
tip/ our hats to marshall allen/
jimmy lyons/ maybe mr. coltrane gone whiz by/
maybe not/ cd be an itinerant errant one-man-negro-
band
over to Grand Central/ but
       we all/ come gallopin out the heavens
to our mothers' bellies/ & the niggah
blue night/ you was wendin yo way
down heah/ *stars fell over alabama/ mood indigo*
new grass/ ornithology/ ascension/ freedom now/
crosstown traffic
& *"i wonder who's lovin you"*/ *"better stop doggin me*
around"
"blase"/ say hey/ *"friends & neighbors"*/ *"doncha*
know you make me wanna
       shout" flew/ out yr mother's mouth
      you/ burst out her body
     & that's how/ you come to be
     a reed man/

loosening strings or give me an 'A'

yes/ i listened to country joe & the fish/
   yes/ i howled with steppenwolf/
yes/ fleetwood mac was my epiphany/
  & creedance clearwater revival
swept me neath the waters/   hendrix
my national anthem always/ yes
   blind lemon jefferson & b. b. huddle
by my stage door/ yes chuck berry lives
next to me/ yes
     eric clapton made me wanna have
         a child named layla/ yes
sonny sharrock drew screams outta me
         linda can't eclipse/
yes/ i remember My Lai & the Audubon debacle
yes/ hamza-el-din is a caracole out my mouth
yes/ i never forgot where i came from &
nobody misses me cuz/
         i never left
  in search of a portrait
     of an artist
       as a yng man/
yes   i read ULYSSES & he came home
        yes/ oh/ yes
           i know my/ Joyce
i cd tell niggah chords meant for me/
yes/ "I searchin . . . I'm searchin"/ my Olympics say
Circe/ the Scylla the Charybdis/
        any Siren & all the Pentagon
yes/ Circe/ the Scylla/ the Charybdis,
   any Siren/ and alla the Pentagon/
aint kept/ yes/ i say/ aint kept

this one/ yes/ niggah man/ from/ yes
                    makin art outta me/
yes/
    "i'm gonna love him all over/ all over/
        & over & over"
cuz niggahs aint in search of/
    we/ just get discovered
so/ yes
  i must be the New World now/ yes
i'm in tune
oh/ yes/ play me
                pick/ my colored tones
  yes/ strum my niggah/ chords
                find/ my sharps & flats
let em/ have/ space
oh/ yes oh/ yes/ i know my Joyce
& Ulysses/ he done come home
yes/ play me/ now
yes/ make me alla that
yes/ i'll be the bottom or i cd just ride
yes/ i know my Joyce/ & all you gotta say/ is
    "Give me a 'A'"
    Ahhhhhhhhhhhhhhhh
yes/ Ulysses he done come home
yes/ i must be the New World
yes/ Ulysses he done come home
yes/ i must be the New World
yes/ i'm in tune
just/ yes/ oh yes/ just play me
  baby/ play me/
                yes/

mesl (male english as a second language): in defense of bilingualism

i watch black & white movies the way
    yall hanker after the World Series
not like i'm on first base or nothin
    & i surely won't be pitchin
but i do know how to walk em or
        bring in three wit one hit to the far
outfield

yeah.

i hadda brother & he showed me some things.

but
i learnt what i know bout game-playin
    on saturdays fore dawn on reruns
        of who for you are Jim Brown & Willie Mays/
    when i fly i don't condense to a pigskin
ellipse or a leather suited billiard ball
    popped outta Yankee Stadium
who for you is ecstasy on Wrigley Field
    is Tyrone Power as Zorro
        Ronald Coleman seekin out the
    Guillotine for my honor
not my chastity or my reputation/
        Ronald Coleman's deliberately
riskin himself cuz/ he loved me so
just on accounta he had offered himself
        to me/
he'd die
    fore that gift was took from me.

there are no umpires/ in my game
    & no men in lil striped shirts/ usin
      sign language
        deaf women don't understand/

hey/

we go for broke/ where i suit up/ but
        i caint say 'xactly where that is
less/ i buy me 19 acres & some astroturf/
      yall got no clarity/ bout what game
        it is we playin.

so/
i'ma talk to you the best i can/
awright/

here's the whole/ 9/ yards/
    i'm the black queen/ but
  that don't make this chess/ cuz
kings don't hold no sway here/ like pawns
  they come & go/
          this aint football/ cuz men
        whose faces i caint see/ don't get
close enough to me/ to tackle nothin/
    & i'm not the quarterback/ cuz
    low-riders don't waste alla they
  hydraulic wizardry/ on nothin
that aint a whole lotta somethin/
    i cd be a goalie/ but why i'm
gone stand round myself wit a crooked stick?
& i have no desire/ to bounce balls
  offa my head/ in fronta
    thousands of people

when i swim
  i'm not aimin for the other side/
  i'm warm waters/ inchin thru coral
lookin to galavant/ on a dolphin's back.

what's the rush abt?

        you caint make a dolphin into a gazelle
        in less than 30,000 years/
    if i take my time
i might come upon Shangri-la/ Mt. Fuji
                        long fore yall gotta
                        national holiday for
Satchel Paige
                    or convince the five
percenters
                    they aint the only ones goin
to Heaven/
                    while they mock Malcom & call
alla
            the rest of us/ they "earths"

whatchu think you standin on?

Diamonds?
Diamonds/ deep in South Africa/ or Chicago?
        you think you are really
        on the Stairway
            to Heaven?
    that/ you the decidin factor/ in
            overtime/ hey

did you ever go to the movies/
      & know
   you/ the hero?

(i caint be no Scarlet/ if you caint find Charleston/ &
the Blue Dahlia/ aint nothin but another bar/ less
you give me
them flowers/ & Sally caint meet Harry/ or Tom or
Dick/
til you ready/ for a feature film)
this/ is really the bottom line.

     i love/ black & white movies/
that's/ the world i was born to/ alla
       them pastel circles round/ neptune/
    rose quartz moon's flirtin wit saturn/
  rouge hues over mars/
 are outer space to me/

& i do/ wanna play wit you/

  i don't wanta win/ necessarily/
   that'd be nice/ but it's how you
say/ "engagée"/ that stirs me & scares you/

in my ballpark/ nobody's decimated/ nobody's
    a loser/   but
it can get rough/

(we cd leave the Astrodome/ in alla our regalia/ &
nobody'd
know/
no/ where
no/ way

who'd won or lost
what)
but/
    they'd know somethin happened/
there was some back breakin/ knee twistin/
shoulder dislocatin/ leapin gainst the
leftfield fence/ shin-splintin/ bitin dust/
umpire cursin/ slidin into home
fandangle/

        oh/
        they'd know/

that's/ how i play
        that's how i play/ everything/

but/ you say/
    "everything seems to work out
        when we talk it over in bed"

hum/

if you cd slam-dunk it/ maybe i'd
        rush the goalposts carryin blue satin/
        string the basket wit red silk/
        ·oil yr body wit mine/

HEY/ HEY/ WHAT D'YA SAY/
        wit some discipline/ 9-3-36-41/
GOOD GOD?
        you might even match my stayin power!
OOOOOOOH . . . let's see/ that/ again/ slowly/
        frame by frame/ imagine that backhand/ pass/
why isaiah thomas/ cdn't have asked for a more/

perfect/ YES
    this is America's genius . . .
can you/
    did you ever see that move?
      have/
you ever seen that/ kind of co-or-di- . . .
did you catch that?
  cd you see?

OOOOOOOOHHHHHHHHHHHHHHHHHH!
whatta game/

hey/

do you wanna play wit me?

devotion to one lover or another

i bathe in gardenia scented
water/ amaryllis fricia & white tulips
move-to-&-from me the way brazen niggahs
what cd dance do when it suit them/ flower
petals lavender coral ivory *rojo amarillo pretu/*
yes/ black petals/ float & open like i do when
i am a devoted lover/ my baths are rituals
like cock crows & cornbread/ but aint a
lover i been devoted to ever known/ thought
abt/ bothered/ or imagined what kinda flowers
should creep over my breasts/ the bubbles & steam
cleanse me of all extraneous energies/ dirt
the earth forces her ravenous scent outta
me/ less i halfway fricassee my definitively
sensate geechee body/ hot hot waters gotta
seduce my muscles/ stretch me/ exorcize
them toxins/ the flower petals
carry danger way from me
this method of survival
has yet to be detected/

it's a pity no one has ever thought
to put you in a tub of flowers
where yr loveliness/ niggah/
is unencumbered/
just steamin
now/ how to stay clean/
we all know white folks
carry lice/ but the world is fulla vermin
what'll kill a something fragile as a love/ & yes
we had good times/ they was beauty there/

so startlin/ as to obscure the veritable north star
but i am not awash in lovers/ quite like that/
it's the ones i cursed/ threw bottles at/ &
plain made myself a ravin fool over/ they
understand my survival/ that i'm still here/
that/ whatever inarticulate desires
we rocked & rolled jus haveta stop demandin
so much/ but that yen to touch/ that
upper lip ever so/ feel yr head up under
them arms/ that/
don't go away/ it stops askin are you awready?
even if i/ kicked him down the stairs/
threw all the damn horns out the window/
that there yen for that touch/ don't care/
& it's time to take a bath/
bedrock don't grow orchids/
i wanna be washed in white tulips/
scarlet amaryllis/ & gardenias/
muthahfuckahs jus caint/ get this together/
i even know some body who wdn't run my water/
& it don't matter to me none/ if
you do think i'm out my rightful mind/
        i say/ lovin is more than pleasurin/
which cd run off with any sense you got/
cause/ devotion is sustenance/
& i know what cleans me/ feeds me/
flowers
earth's offered up/ so beautifully
they can float off from me/ with
all this dirt/
we colored & in love/
we in mortal danger/
i don't bathe in wild flowers/ for nothin/

"if i go all the way without you
where would i go?"

—The Iseley Brothers

there/ to the right of venus
                close to where yr lion
stalks our horizon/   see/
listen/
glow scarlet/ char-scarlet/ set my heart down
there/   near you/ scaldin *amarillo*/
oh/ say/ my new day
                my dawn/
yr fingers trace the rush of my lips/
                ever so reverent/
                ever so hungry/

here/
to the right side of venus/
                my tongue/
                tropical lightenin/
rush/ now/ softly/ tween my toes/ the seas ebb
& in these sands/ i've come back/
                an unpredictible swell
a fresh water lily/ in the north atlantic/
when you touch me/   yes
that's how pearls somehow/ rip from the white of my
bones
    to yr fingertips/
    incontrovertible hard chicago/
                rococo implications/
& this/   the mississippi delta/ tween my thighs
yr second touch/ forbids
a thing less/ than primordial fluidity/

no/
i lay next to you/
          the undertow at carmel/
the russian river/ feelin up stalks of the best/ of
humboldt county
& damn it/
          what makes you think/ my spine is
yr personal/
san andreas fault?

                    shiftin/ serene fields break for rain/
til
i open/ deep brown moist & black
          cobalt sparklin everywhere/
we are
there/
          where the pacific fondles my furthest
shores/ detroit-high-russet/ near redwoods/
          i am climbin
                    you chase me/ from limb to limb/
                              pullin/ the colored stars/ out the
night
                              slippin em/ over my tongue/
&
i thought i cd get over/
the dangers/ of livin
          on the pacific rim/
when i look at you/
i
know/ i am riskin my life/
     tossin reason/ to the outback of the far
rockaways/
                    goin/ givin up/ everything/ with out
protest/

givin up/ meteorological episodes
the appalachian mountains/
                    handin over/ islands from puget
sound/
                    travis county hill country/
givin away/ treasures/
i
never
claimed/
      til i felt you/

my own december sunset/ teasin cypress/
even campbell street bikers/ in downtown oakland/
i stopped resistin/
what won't/ be orderly/ imagined/ legitimate/
yes/ yes/
hold me
like/ the night grabs wyoming/
& i am more/ than i am not/
i cd sing sacred lyrics/ to songs i don't know/
my cheek/ rubs gainst the nappy black/ cacti of yr
chest/
& i am a flood/ of supernovas/
if you kiss me like that/ i'm browned wetlands
yr lips/ invite the moon/ to meander/
our mouths open & sing/
yes/
our tongues/
the edge of the earth/

I Heard Eric Dolphy in His Eyes

"I Heard Eric Dolphy in His Eyes," is a performance piece designed to explore the violence and lyricism, the incongruities and the constants, as well as the magic and limitations of Afro-American urban life and our music that documents our realities and sometimes impossible yearnings for peaceful, nurturing actualities.

The company of six (three musicians, three dancer/actresses) explicates the exigencies of reality versus possibility through five monologues and four dance sequences; all involve interaction with the musicians as well as fragments of Dolphy compositions and solos. The rhythms and language of the monologues compells the movement and music that lead us to the next spoken words. Some things fall easily into speech, while others defy verbal exegesis, available only through music, and the fluid or percussive eloquence of the human body in motion.

i heard eric dolphy in his eyes

yesterday evenin/ no/ mo like last night/ the
moon took on a scarlet hue/ *lune rouge/ luna
roja/ una luna loca/ soy yo una loquita/*
thru mists & the clouds that mix
wit neon invitations & tears unshed/ tears
waitin for tomorrow/ i met the 7th Avenue IRT
Express/ specially tailored for Malcolm X Boulevard
& the computerized palettes at the
Schomberg/ the train came whistling by/ deluxe
from 145th Street/ to my heart/ throbbin
& seekin rhythms not uncomfortable wit wind
chill factors & smog what cd mix wit neon &
cloud/ hoverin/ by the base of hydrants
ferocious brazen legs of young girls seein to
their own undoin/
    "Rah, Rah"
i says/ is this a football game
    "Rah, Rah"

i says/ the Knicks must be playin at
155th Street/ in the chill spill of the night/
    "Rah, Rah"
the march/ is movin on to Howard Beach/
another day/ of outrage/
    "Rah, Rah"
must be Daniel Ortega/ or Fidel/ back
on a terrace/ wit confetti & chicken
feathers/ cheers of absolution/
cheers/ proclaimin the comin/ of
a new day/
    "Rah, Rah"

come a voice/ pummelin/ like a
bulldozer/ come a voice too usedta pain/
    "Rah, Rah"
the child's tumblin/ from one pole to
the next/ his filthy tattered snowsuit
mo accustomed/ to bein spat on/
than makin angels/ the cold nibbles his
naked lil feet/ he cries/ this baby who can
barely walk/ cuz he simply
is too young/ now/ the child cries & smiles
at the same time/ deaf to his own name/
    "Rah, Rah"
                  "niggah/ get up off da floor/ ya heah
me?
                  git yo black ass off da floor/ niggah/ ya
heah me?"
the child/ RahRah/ shoulda been
praised/ he tries so hard/ he tries
he tries/ so hard/ he reaches/ wit his lil
arms for the hard grey plastic of the
subway bench/ he pulls his pink-smudged feet
up/ offa the ground/ but/ not fast enough
cuz the voice/ that barrelin
crude/ nasty ol voice/ keeps chasin the
child/ up & up & up/ to the seat/ &
then/ the po child falls back down/ on
top the comic strips from the *Daily News*/ the
Times OpEd page/ the personals from *The Advocate*/
& miscellaneous/ spiritual opportunities featured in
the *Amsterdam News*/ proclaimin that only
one/ Papa Legbé visited Harlem each
year/ & only one/ love could save us from
misfortune/ & only one/ child was
hoisted by the seat of his pants/ nose

first down on the hard littered
bench/ where the hand of the voice
the fist of the low-down muthafuckah
crashed into the flesh & marrow of a child
who can barely talk/ or walk/ who has mastered
the art of weepin & smilin/ at the
same time/ a child who raises his arms like
like he gonna hug the voice/
    "Rah, Rah"
he's lookin/ at all of us/
the fists/ ricochet off his
temple to his calves/ smilin &
cryin/ wishin/ maybe wishin/ this heah
time/ the voice won't take his dirty red
hat/ offa his scabby nappy head/ wishin
the hands of the voice/ wouldn't roll his
pants legs up/ so wazn't no way to fend off
the cold/ hopin a tambourine/ wouldn't be
set on top his stroller/ by the voice/
takin off his own shoes to balance/ on
a wooden leg/ he leans on it
when he's not beatin/
    "RahRah"
                "we gonna make some money
                tonight/ we gonna git fired up/
                awright/ yeah/ yeah tonight/
                tonight/
                gone git me/ all fired up/
                tonight"
& whack/ cross the baby's head wit
knuckles/ leavin a puffed up
bleedin space/ neath the right eye/
& the baby tries to smile/

"ladies & gentlemen/ we heah is
homeless & we'd like ya to give
us/ whatever the lord moves ya
to do/ ya know how kids are/
sometimes/ ya gotta be a lil
hard on em"
speak to me/ RahRah/ speak to me/
RahRah/ i wanna sing to ya til
there's/ no mo fog round lake michigan/
til there's/ no mo steely cacophony
just above yo head/ let ya
breathe somethin tender/ like dew/ fresh
air & someone tenderly round bout
ya/ everywhere/ i swear i heard A.I.R.
delicately triumph/ in his eyes/
tender in his eyes/ fierce/ in his eyes
i say/ i heard an A.I.R. song

i heard A.I.R. in his eyes/
RahRah/ RahRah/
i heard please/ in his sighs
i heard/ what'd i ever do to you/ in his eyes
RahRah/ RahRah/
Get up/ run for yo life/

there in his eyes in the harsh
night/ trail of whimpers & mean giggles
led a solo bassoon/ a
bass clarinet/ some sound broader mo
powerful/ than this child/ i know/ i heard
Chicago howlin thru his eyes/ when
love surfaces like crumbs/ he's
gone set up & grin/ i knew ya were heah
all along/ ya were heah/ like

me/ unfinished & frail/ like an A.I.R.
song/ rockin/ sadness/

i wanna know/ what love sounds like/
i wanna know/ what love sounds like
A.I.R./ fresh air/ new A.I.R./ in his eyes/
Rah Rah/ Rah Rah/
i hear don't hit me again awright
in his eyes/ cold or night/ in his eyes/
RahRah/ RahRah/
i heard/ eric dolphy in his eyes/

> "ladies and gentlemen/ we heah is
> homeless & we'd like ya to give
> us/ whatever the lord moves ya
> to do/ ya know how kids are/
> sometimes/ ya gotta be a lil
> hard on em"

crack annie

i caint say how it come to me/ shit
somehow/ it just come over me/ & i
heard the lord sayin how beautiful/ &
pure waz this child of mine/ & when i
looked at her i knew the Lord waz
right/ & she waz innocent/ ya know/
free of sin/ & that's how come i
gave her up to cadillac lee/ well/ how
else can i explain it/

who do ya love i wanna know i wanna know
who do ya love i wanna know i wanna know

what mo could i say

who do ya love i wanna know i wanna know
who do ya love i wanna know i wanna know

it's not like she had hair round her
pussy or nothin/ she ain't old enough
anyway for that/ & we sho know/ she
aint on the rag or nothin/ but a real
good friend of mine from round 28th
street/ he tol me point-blank
wazn't nothin in the whole world smell
like virgin pussy/ & wazn't nothin in the
universe/ taste like new pussy/ now this
is my friend talkin/ & ya know how
hard it is to keep a good man fo yo self
these days/ even though i know i got
somethin sweet & hot to offer/ even

then/ i wanted to give my man cadillac
lee/ somethin i jus don't have no mo/
new pussy/ i mean it aint dried up or
nothin/ & i still know what muscles i
cd get to work in my pussy/ this-a-way
& that but what i really wanted/ my
man/ cadillac to have for his self/ waz some
new pussy/ & berneatha waz so
pretty & sweet smellin/ even after
she be out there runnin wit the boys/
my berneatha *vida*/ waz sweet & fine
remember that song "so fine"
 so fine my baby's so doggone fine
 sends them thrills up & down my spine
whoah-oh-oh-yeah-yeaeaeah-so-fine

well/ that's my child/ *fine*/ & well
cadillac always come thru for me/ ya
know wit my crack/ oh honey/ lemme tell
ya how close to jesus i get thanks
to my cadillac/ lemme say now/ witout
that man i'd been gone on to
worms & my grave/ but see i had me
some new pussy/ waz my daughter/ lemme
take that back/ i didn't have none/
any new pussy/ so i took me some/ & it
jus happened to be berneatha/ my
daughter/ & he swore he'd give me twenty-five
dollars & a whole fifty cent of crack/
whenever/ i wanted/ but you know/ i'm on the pipe/
& i don't have no new pussy/ & what difference/
could it
make/ i mean shit/ she caint get pregnant/
shit/ she only seven years old

& these scratches/ heah/ by my fingers
that's/ where my child held onto
me/ when the bastard/ cadillac/ took
her like she wazn't even new pussy at
all/ she kept lookin at me &
screamin/ "mommy/ mommy help me/ help
me"/ & all i did waz hold her
tighter/ like if i could stop her
blood from circulation/ if i could stop
her from hurtin/ but no/ that aint how
it went down at all/ nothin like that/
trust me/ i got scars where my
daughter's fingernails broke my skin
& then/ when he waz finished wit my
child/ cadillac/ he jump up & tell me
to cover my child's pussy/ wit some
cocaine/ so she wdn't feel nothin no
mo/ i say/ why ya aint done
that befo/ why ya wait til ya done/
to protect her/ he say/ befo i lay
you down & give ya some of the same/
dontcha know/ ya haveta hear
em scream befo ya give em any
candy/ & my lil girl heard all
this/ my child bled alla this/ & all i
could do waz to look for some more crack
wit the fifty cadillac done give
me/ but/ i wazn't lookin for it for
me/ jesus knows/ i wanted it for
berneatha/ so she wouldn't haveta
remember/ she wouldn't have to
remember/ nothin at all/ but i saw dark purple
colored marks
by her shoulder/ where i held her down for

cadillac/ i'm her mother & i held her
& if ya kill me/ i'll always know/
i'm gonna roam round hell talkin
bout new pussy/ & see my child's
blood caked bout her thighs/ my child's
shoulders purple wit her mother's
love/ jesus save me/ come get me
jesus/ now/ lord take my soul & do
wit it what ya will/ lord have
mercy/ i thought berneatha waz like
me/ that she could take anythin/ ya
know/ caint nothin kill the will of the
colored folks/ but lord i waz
wrong/ them marks on my child/ no/
not the marks/ from cadillac/ the scars
from my fingers/ purple & blue
blotches/ midnight all ruby on lenox
avenue at 7:30 on sundays/ that heavy
quiet/ that cruelty/ i caint take
no mo/ so lord throw me into hell befo
berneatha is so growed/ she do it
herself/ all by herself/ laughin
& shovin me/ & prowlin &
teasin/ sayin/ you a mother/ what
kinda mother are you/ bitch/ tell me/
now/ mommy what kinda mother/ are you/ mommy/
mommy/

i say/ i heard etta james in her eyes/ i
know/ i heard the blues in her eyes/ an
unknown/ virulent blues/ a stalkin

takin no answer but yes to me
blues/ a song of a etta james/ a
cantankerous blues/ a blues born of
wantin & longin/ wantin & longin for
you/ mama/ or etta mae/
song of a ol hand me down blues
hangin by its breath/ alone
a fragile new blues
hardly close to nowhere/ cept them eyes
& i say/ i heard a heap of etta james
in them eyes/ all over them eyes/
so come on Annie

so tell mama all about it

tell mama all about it
all about it
all about it

tell mama

running backwards/ conroe to canarsie

i.

before i was born
they said/ the Scottsboro Boys did it/
when/ i was a child/
they said/ Emmett Till did it/
now/ i'ma woman/
and my child's a child/
and they say/ Clarence Brandley did it/

some/ one of them/
some black boy/ or man/
who didn't bow his head/ or grin with teeth/
or jus was in the vicinity of/ or
with access to/ or imagined/ access
to the now/ dead white girl/
glorified/ in her decay/
sanctified/ in her
demise/
closer to God in death/ than in life/

a niggah did it/
had to be/
the Lord smite evil out the hands
of white folks/
that's how come/ they know/
a niggah did it/
ask any/ white man/ in Conroe/

Run niggah Run!   Got me a niggah this
I got ya this time!   time.
   Hey, Niggah!   Can ya hear me, boy!
   That's right, niggah   Over here!
                                    Right here!
          I been waitin for this a long time.

ii.

we's eatin pizza at the pizza shop/
when we see's these niggahs/ at the
counter talkin like they's gonna eat
some pizza too/ this/ is our
neighborhood!/ we don't have no trash in
the streets/ and niggers in the pizza
parlor at nighttime/ there's decent folks
around here & white women & my
children/ how we gonna let some niggers/
just walk in & walk out of where we
live/ like they hadda right to go
wherever they wanted to go/ so/ we
jammed em up/ ya know/ with some sticks
& tire irons & baseball bats
& our fists/ we chased em/ like runnin dogs/
cause a nigger's got to know/ not to come
around Howard Beach/ Bernard Goetz was
right/ he's my hero/ ya know/ get em
before they get you/ cause once ya let
one in/ you can't stop it/ they're like
roaches/ they come out at night.

iii.

Hey Niggah! Over here!
That's right, niggah. Right here!
I been waitin for this a long time. Got me a
Run, niggah, run! niggah this
I got ya this time! time.
Can ya hear
me, boy?

iv.

hush now/ don't explain
there's nothin to gain
i'm glad you're back
don't explain

did you have a black boy for his neck to
be broke/ for his father to see forsook
tell me/ cuz i wanna know/
hush now/ don't explain
you're my joy & pain
my life/ your love
don't explain

now/ somebody needs to tell me why/ my
boy's gotta die/ deep in some river/
we 'magine flowin to heaven/ oh oh . . . *hush*
now/ yo child aint to
blame/ less he gotta sign

writ all up & down his berry black back
say what/ say/ cicatrix are improvised
these days/ Lord/ Lord come by heah/
this/ is the word of God/ & we a God's
children/ this heah/ is the new Jerusalem/
& apartheid is a mortal sin/ teach me/ Jesus/
tell somebody to say that/ in Crown Heights/
find me a witness/ to croon roundabout/ Howard
Beach/ that the Lord God Almighty/ done sent
his children a message/ yes/ Jesus/ lookin
now/ for an eye for an eye/ & a tooth for a tooth/
best don't let no guinea/ let his mouth be loose/
                    hush now don't explain

i caught the Lady/ in my man's eyes
heard her tossin in his torment/ i heard Billie
Holiday in his touch/ whenever we thought
of the boy we loved so much.
                    hush now don't explain

give me an ax/ give me a machete/
get me a 9-millimeter machine gun &
just look at me/ til i see/
i say/ who/ i heard in yo eyes/
i say/ i heard Charles Mingus/
in his eyes.

open up/ this is the police

Open up this is the police
Open up/ you hear.

*mira/ mira/ negra la policía viene
toma la coca/ toma la coca/ ahorita Inez
toma la coca/ la policia viene/*

now/ heah i am 8 months gone/ 8 months
pregnant/ & i gonna swallow a ounce
of cocaine/ cuz he say . . .

*mira/ mira/ toma la coca
mira/ mira/ toma la coca*

. . . cuz i'm afraid/ man/ &
we'll all be separated/ i'll go to
the joint/ & there'll be some goddamned
foster parents/ & the social workers & the lawyers &
the judge/ & the AFDC & the child welfare
department/
& i'll go back to Aguas Buenas/ & they'll all say
shit/ wazn't nothin to him/ *maricon
muy mala gente*

mira/ mira/ toma la coca

& then/ maybe i'll have me a heart attack/ &
the medical examiner/ he say/ the baby
done had a heart attack/ too/ & now aint
nobody/ *ningún/* goin nowhere/ but to the chair
cuz the only right to life/ i had
i done killt/ man . . .

Mira/ mira/ toma la coca
Mira/ mira/ toma la coca

cuz my body/ is a a livin tomb/ man
a death threat/ ya get/ whatta mean?

mira/ mira/ toma la coca
mira/ mira/ toma la coca
mira/ mira/ toma la coca

                Git down on the floor/ niggah/ face
                down/ on the floor/
niggah. . . . . . .
        sing me a reggae dirge/ i wanna
        hear/ oh/ sing me now
"i am what i am i am i am i am"/ cuz
i & i/ gonna shoot Peter Tosh tonight/
yeah/ i & i/ gonna cut the light/ right outta his
sight/ tonight/ sing/ me/ now
'i am what i am i am i am i am'
                Down on the floor/
niggah/ face down on the floor/
           sing me
           a
           last
           breath
           reggae/
                niggah
hey/ Peter
sing me/
      a liberation song/

mira/ mira/ toma la coca
mira/ mira/ toma la coca

down on the floor/ face down/ on the floor

        how you like silence/ bro'dah
      how you like/ yo brains blowed out/
   ras' man/ speak to me/
speak up/ niggah

           . . . he didn't mean/ for me to die/ &
           pequeñita esmerelda/ that waz gonna
           be her name/ Esmerelda/ if she was
           a girl
           but/ she waz a girl/ she waz a girl/
           & she dead cuz . . .

mira/ mira/ toma la coca
mira/ mira/ toma la coca

down on the floor/
face down/ on the floor/
          . . . that waz my *novio*
          that waz my child

   "there'll be a burnin & a lootin tonight
   there'll be a burnin & a lootin tonight"

he kept/ sayin/ *negra/ te amo/ escúcheme/*
negrita linda/ inez/ oígame/ te amo/ dime/
dime/ que/ la niña viva/ la niña viva
dígame/ una palabra/
         como amor/
           como siempre/

mira/ mira/ toma la coca
mira/ mira/ toma la coca

down/ on the floor
face down/ on the floor/

       in the womb/ in the dark/ we see so
       little/ we don't know our way round/
       ya see/ but Esmereldita floats cherubic/
       yeah/ in placenta waters/ streams of
       tears
       & *plenas*/ in the Bronx/ say/ Hoboken/
       Esmereldita/ *saba los ritmos* of the
       bata y la pachanga/ but i never saw/
       her eyes
       her eyes/ cuz i never saw her/ eyes
       you'll never see/ her eyes/ we don't
       know what she thinks/ bout the music
       in our blood/ i know/ i hear Arsenio
       Rodriquez in her eyes/ reachin
       desperate fingers/ beggin for life/
       pluck-by-pluck/ while young girls'
       bodies' slide in a hell/ that's no longer
       underground
where Peter Tosh's
head & tongue
are no more/ than
bloody spots/
somewhere/ in Jamaica

       i know/ i hear Arsenio Rodriquez
       in her eyes/

Glossary

A.I.R.—New Black Music Trio composed of Henry Threadgill (reeds), Fred Hopkins (bass), and the late Steve McCall (percussion).

Eric Dolphy—virtuoso reed man from Los Angeles whose clarity and lyricism created new attitudes towards the flute and bass clarinet in music. He died in the mid-sixties while touring Europe. See *Out to Lunch* & *Last Date*.

Charles Mingus—African-American jazz bassist and composer. See *Theme for Lester Young* & *Eat That Chicken Pie*.

Peter Tosh—guitarist, singer, and composer with reggae artist Bob Marley and the original Wailers. He was gunned down in his home in Jamaica by political marauders.

Arsenio Rodriguez—blind, black Cuban composer and cuatro player of signal importance to the development of contemporary salsa as presently understood. See *Routes to Rhythm: Chano Pozo to Ruben Blades*.

About the Author

Ntozake Shange is the author of *for colored girls . . .*, *"Spell #7,"* and *"A Photograph: Lovers in Motion,"* the poetry volumes, *nappy edges, A Daughter's Geography, Ridin' The Moon in Texas,* and *From Okra to Greens.* In addition to her novel, *Sassafrass, Cypress & Indigo,* Ms. Shange has adapted her novel *Betsey Brown* to *Betsey Brown: A Rhythm & Blues Musical* with Emily Mann and Bakida Carroll which will open at the McCarter Theater in the Spring of 1991. *"I heard eric dolphy in his eyes"* will be presented by the Creation for Liberation Theater in London during the Winter Season. Ms. Shange's work-in-progress, *The Love Space Demands: A Continuing Saga,* will be part of the Crossroads Theater Genesis Project this year. Both "I Live in Music" and "Beneath the Necessity of Talking" performed with Ms. Shange's band, Syllable (John Purcell on reeds and Jean-Paul Bourelly on guitars), are available on audio-cassette from the American Audio-Prose Library. Syllable appearing live with Ms. Shange is available on video-cassette from The San Francisco Poetry Center. Ms. Shange has worked and performed with innumerable artists including Dianne McIntyre's Sounds-In-Motion, Raymond Sawyer's

Afro-Asian Dance Company, Ed Mock's West Coast Dance Works, and The Stanze Peterson Dance Company, as well as musicians David Murray, Fred Hopkins, Oliver Lake, Henry Threadgill, Billy Bang, and the late Steve McCall.

Ms. Shange's column appears regularly in Philadelphia's REAL NEWS; articles and poetry may be found in *Uncut Funk, Callaloo, Muleteeth,* and *Essence.*